What the Bible Teaches About Drinking Wine

by
Dr. Bruce Lackey

What the Bible Teaches About Drinking Wine

**Original © Copyright 1985 by
Bruce P. Lackey
3020 Northway Lane
Chattanooga, TN 37406**

Through the ministry of Dr. Bob Green, permission was obtained from Mrs. Helen Lackey, wife of Dr. Bruce Lackey, to republish this booklet by The Old Paths Publications for which we are eternally thankful. No words have been changed, only formatting.

Republished by:
The Old Paths Publications
142 Gold Flume Way
Cleveland, Ga 30528
www.theoldpathspublications.com
TOP@theoldpathspublications.com

ISBN: 978-1-7351454-6-4

July 2020

TABLE OF CONTENTS

What the Bible Teaches About Drinking Wine

Some time ago, the newspapers around the country reported a famous preacher's comment about social drinking. He said, "I do not believe that the Bible teaches teetotalism. I can't; Jesus drank wine. Jesus turned water into wine at a wedding feast. That wasn't grape juice, as some of them try to claim."

Of course, many people have held this view, through the years, but it is a sad day when a man who is noted as a Bible preacher also espouses the same position. So, it is incumbent upon us to look into the Bible itself and see what the scriptures actually teach about the drinking of wine.

Another reason that such a study is so important is that, even though the drinking of hard liquor has decreased, wine consumption has grown by leaps and bounds over the past few years.

In order to arrive at the truth, we must consider the following facts from the Bible.

1. The Bible warns against the misuse of words.

II Peter 2 tells us that, in the last days, we can expect people to twist the words of God. In verse one, Peter says, *"But there were false prophets among the people, even as there shall be false teachers among you."* Then, in verse three, he reveals what their method will be: *"And through covetousness shall they with feigned words make merchandise of you."*

Consider that phrase, *"feigned words."* The word *feigned* simply means "fabricated," or, made to mean what you want it to mean; misused; that is, using a good word, but with a wrong definition. Peter tells us that this method will be used by false teachers to make merchandise of people.

Verse 18 of the same chapter elaborates: *"For when they speak great swelling words of vanity, they allure through the lusts of the flesh... "* The " great swelling words" would be words which have been expanded out of proportion, and have been made to mean something different from what was intended originally.

Those who are familiar with the methods of false cults can testify that this has long

5

been their tactic. They take good Bible words, such as "born again ... salvation ... hell" and re-define them according to their own teaching. So, we can expect this method to be widely used.

2. To learn the meaning of words, we must obey 1 Corinthians 2:13.

The proper meaning of a word as it is found in the Bible can be learned only by comparing scripture with scripture. Sometimes we resort to the definitions that we find in the dictionary, but they may not always be biblical. We must remember that dictionary definitions have to do with the current usage of a word. But, by looking up a word in a concordance as it appears in several places in scripture, we can arrive at a true, biblical definition. That is the very principle which is taught in 1 Corinthians 2:13 , when it says *"Which things also we speak, not in the words which man's wisdom teacheth, but which the Holy Ghost teacheth; comparing* spiritual *things with spiritual."* Because of this, a good concordance is invaluable in the study of the Word of God.

3. Some words in the Bible are generic (that is, general, not specific).

Genesis 1:29 gives us a good

example: "meat." When we think of meat, we normally think of flesh: some type of ham, or beef, or fish; but when the Bible uses it, in many places it simply means food. In this verse, it obviously means food, not flesh, since it says that *"every herb bearing seed...every tree, in the which is the fruit of a tree yielding seed"* is meat! Verse 30 has the same meaning: *"I have given every green herb for meat."*

The same idea is given in Leviticus 2, where God gave the law about the meat offering. Verse one says that it should be *"of fine flour."* He is clearly talking about some kind of bread or cake that would be made, then have oil and frankincense poured upon it, after which they were to bake it and offer it before the Lord. The meaning is food, not flesh.

John 4:32 has the same usage, when the Lord Jesus said, *"I have meat to eat that ye know not of."*

In like manner, corn is a generic word. Properly, what we call corn is maize, but our modern usage limits the meaning of the word. Originally, corn was a generic word for all kinds of grain. Several scriptures show this. Numbers 18:27 speaks of the *"corn of the threshing floor."* As every farmer knows, you do not thresh corn, you pull it. Wheat, oats, and other grains are threshed, Thus, the Bible is using "corn" in the generic sense.

Job 24:24 mentions *"the tops of the ears of corn."* Of course; the ears of maize do not grow on the tops of the stalks; he is referring to some kind of grain such as wheat or oats, where the kernels do grow on the top.

The most convincing verse is John 12:24, *"Except a corn of wheat ..."* I had difficulty with this for many years, because I did not understand that corn is a generic term. I thought of it only as maize. We would say, in the twentieth century, "except a grain of wheat."

Thus we have seen two generic words: meat and corn. We might also have mentioned beer, cidet; cereal; and many others.

I submit that the Biblical word *wine* is also generic. It means **"the juice of the grape,"** whether it be new or old, fermented or unfermented, alcoholic or non- alcoholic. Sometimes, it definitely means fresh grape juice. The following pages will give us clear instances in which we may determine its specific meaning.

8

4. The word "wine" sometimes means fresh juice.

Deuteronomy 11:14 says, *"I will give you the rain of your land in his due season; the first rain and the latter rain, that thou mayest gather in thy corn, and the wine, and thine oil."* Everyone knows that a person does not gather alcoholic wine from the vine. Even if the grape rotted on the vine, the juice would be sour, acidic vinegar-wine, rather than alcoholic. Therefore, when this scripture speaks of gathering their wine, it means gathering fresh juice!

I Chronicles 31:5 is similar. *"The children of Israel brought in abundance the first fruits of corn, wine, and oil, and honey and of all the increase of the field."* The word *ftrstfruits* shows that they brought in the very first things that became ripe. Also, the verse begins with the words, *"As soon as the commandment came abroad, the children of Israel brought in ... "* There was no time for an aging process which would turn grape juice into alcoholic wine; he calls it wine!

Nehemiah 13:15 has the same meaning. *"In those days saw I in Judah some treading wine presses on the sabbath."* They were squeezing the juice

9

from the grapes, yet he called it a wine press. Everyone knows that one does not get alcoholic wine from squeezing grapes!

Proverbs 3:10 promises, *"... thy presses shall burst out with new wine."* If one could get alcoholic wine from newly picked grapes, people would not spend a lot of money building expensive distilleries and studying the best ways of wine-making. When scripture mentions wine coming from the wine-press, it obviously means fresh grape juice.

Isaiah 16: 10 is similar: *"The treaders shall tread out no wine in their presses."*

Isaiah 65:8 goes even further: *"As the new wine is found in the cluster... "* Everyone knows that there is no alcoholic beverage while the juice is still in the grape! Wine 1s generic; here, it means fresh grape juice.

Jeremiah 48:33 has the same meaning: *"I have caused wine to fail from the winepresses."*

I Timothy 5:23 seems to be a problem to many people, when Paul advises Timothy to *"drink no longer water, but a little wine for thy stomach's sake and thine often infirmities."* Many insist that here, the Bible gives the privilege, if not a command, of using wine (alcoholic) as a medicine. However, this can not possibly be referring to alcoholic wine. The reason? Because he specifically says that it is to be drunk for Timothy's stomach's sake. He obviously had some kind of stomach disease and any doctor will tell you that such a person must abstain from alcoholic beverage. This author has had much stomach trouble through the years and has consulted various doctors, observing various dietary restrictions. In every case, they warned against drinking any alcoholic beverage whatsoever. If we know that today, surely the Holy Spirit of God knew that when He inspired this verse!

We do not know what Timothy's specific infirmities were, nor do we know what kind of healing properties there were in grape juice. Maybe Paul was saying that Timothy should not drink the water, since in many parts of the world it is not pure and would cause a healthy person to have trouble from amoebas, etc. One who already had stomach problems would only multiply them by drinking impure water. Paul might have been recommending that Timothy drink grape juice only. In any case, we can be positive that he was not telling him to put alcohol in a bad stomach!

5. The context will always show when "wine" refers to alcoholic beverage.

In such cases, God discusses the bad effects of it and warns against it. An example would be Genesis 9, Noah's experience after the flood. Verse 21, *"And he drank of the wine, and was drunken..."* clearly means alcoholic beverage.

Proverbs 20:1 speaks of the same thing when it warns us, *"Wine is a mocker, strong drink is raging; and whosoever if deceived thereby is not wise."* Alcoholic wine is deceptive; but how? In the very way that people are advocating today, by saying that drinking a little bit will not hurt. Everyone admits that drinking too much is bad; even the liquor companies tell us not to drive and drink, but they insist that a small amount is all right. However, that is the very thing that is deceptive; who knows how little to drink? Experts tell us that each person is different. It takes an ounce to affect one, while more is necessary for another. But, the same person will react to alcohol differently, depending on the amount of food he has had, among other things. So, the idea that "a little bit won't hurt" is deceptive, and whosoever is deceived thereby is not wise!

Proverbs 23:30-31 refers to alcoholic wine, because it tells us in the previous verse that those who drink it have woe, sorrow, contentions, babbling, wounds without cause, and redness of eyes. What a graphic description of those who "tarry long" at alcoholism. Verses 32-35 continue the same description; context always makes it clear when alcohol is meant.

But if "wine" may mean fresh grape Jmce or alcohol, how can we ever know which? This should not be confusing. In our language, we have various words which have two or even three meanings. For instance, the word "story," according to Webster's Dictionary, may mean (1) the telling of a happening, (2) a falsehood or fib, (3) a section or horizontal division of a building. Suppose a foreigner were to read these three definitions and wonder, "How can I ever know what it means? Which definition would apply?" The obvious answer to that question is to see how the word is used in a sentence. "I live on the third story," obviously means something different from "He told me an interesting story." The context determines! So it is in the Bible. We can tell when "wine" means fresh grape juice and when it means alcoholic beverage, by reading the context, just as we have done in the previous paragraphs.

6. Scripture warns against the drinking of alcoholic wine.

The Bible is consistent on this, in both the Old and New Testaments. The two previously quoted passages, Proverbs 20:1 and 23:29-35, are good examples of scriptural warnings against the consuming of alcohol. Verse 32 says *"at the last it biteth like a serpent, and stingeth like an adder."* Verse 33 shows that it will cause one to look at strange women (that is, not one's wife) and to say perverse things, or things which he would not say if he were sober. Verse 34 predicts that it will cause death, such as drowning, or loneliness, such as lying upon the top of a mast, Verse 35 warns against numbness *("they have beaten me and I felt it not")* and addiction *("when shall I awake? I will seek it yet again")*.

Proverbs 31:4-5 teaches, *"It is not for kings, 0 Lemuel, it is not for kings to drink wine; nor for princes strong drink: lest they drink and forget the law, and pervert the judgment of any of the*

14

afflicted." The danger is obvious.

By the way, verses 6-7 in this chapter give us the only legitimate use of alcoholic wine, in scripture. *"Give strong drink unto him that is ready to perish, and wine unto those that be of heavy hearts. Let him drink, and forget his poverty, and remember his misery no more."* This would be using it as an analgesic; a pain-killer. But this is not for everyone; he says in verse 6, *"unto him that is ready to perish."* Of course, they did not have all the pain-killers that we have today. In our time, it would not be necessary to do this. We have many analgesics available for those who are dying. Then, about the only thing available to the average person would have been some kind of alcohol. Alcohol is a depressant; it is not a stimulant, as some think. After several drinks, one gets dizzy; then he will pass out. So, this passage teaches that alcoholic beverage would be only for the person who is ready to die; there would be no hope for his life. All that would be possible would be to ease his pain and help him forget his misery.

Another passage is Isaiah 5:11, *"Woe unto them that rise up early in the morning, that they may follow strong drink; that continue until night, till wine inflame them!"* Obviously, this is alcoholic, because it inflames. Why does he say "Woe unto them?" Verse 12 answers, *"...they regard not the work of the Lord, neither consider the operation of his hands."* Everyone knows that, when one gives himself to the drinking of beverage alcohol, he will not be more spiritual, not hungry for God, not desirous of learning the Word of God; to the contrary, it causes a person to ignore the Lord. But, verses 13-14 reveal two other serious results: people go into captivity (become slaves to something or someone) and hell enlarges herself! The drinking of alcoholic wine has caused hell to be enlarged! God does not want anyone to go to hell; He has given the greatest, dearest gift that He possibly could, to rescue sinners from it. He never made hell for people, in the first place. The Lord Jesus, Himself, said that hell was prepared for the devil and his angels (Matthew 25:41). However, because of evil alcohol, including alcoholic wine, hell has had an enlargement campaign. Here, then is a clear warning against drinking alcohol, because God does not want anyone to go to hell.

Isaiah 28:7-8 continues the warning. *"But*

they also have erred through wine, and through strong drink are out of the way: the priest and the prophet have erred through strong drink, they are swallowed up of wine, they are out of the way through strong drink; they err in vision, they stumble in judgment. For all tables are full of vomit and filthiness, so that there is no place clean."

What a tragic thing, that even in the days of Isaiah, the priests and prophets were engaged in the drinking of alcoholic wine! Thus, we see that the problem of preachers recommending alcohol is not new. Six hundred years before Christ, demon alcohol had worked its way into religion.

7.   Alcoholic wine is not the result of a natural process.

So many people think it is! I also thought it, years ago, having heard people say so and assuming that it was true. I took for granted, that, if you took the juice of a grape and let it alone, not refrigerating it, it would automatically, in time, turn into alcoholic wine. There are several reasons why that is not true. First, why do men build such expensive distilleries in order to make wine? Why not just get some gallon jugs, fill them with grape juice, and wait?

The answer is obvious. It takes more than time to make wine. Common sense, then proves that alcohol is not the result of a natural process. It would follow, therefore, that God did not make alcohol. Sometimes people try to defend its use by saying that it must be good because God made it. But, the fact is, God did not make it. Man has learned how to do so, through processes that he invented.

Second, wine-makers know that one must have the correct amounts of water, sugar, and temperature in order to make wine. Keeping grape juice in a refrigerator would prevent it from fermenting, because the temperature is not right. Likewise, hot, tropical temperature would prevent it.

Everyone knows that those who produce alcoholic beverage must use sugar. Likewise, the correct consistency of water must be present. In ancient days, before we had refrigeration and vacuum-sealing ability, people learned how to preserve the juice of the grape without its turning into alcoholic wine. Many people in the middle east, Greece, and Rome, would take the juice and boil it down into a thick syrup. By doing so, they could preserve it for long periods of time. When they got ready to drink it, they would simply add the water back to the consistency desired, in much the same way that we take frozen concentrates and add water. In Bible days, contrary to what many believe, the people who wanted to preserve the juice so that they would not have to make it wine knew how to do it. It was not necessary for everyone to drink alcoholic wine as a table beverage, as some would insist.

I recommend the book entitled *"Bible Wines And The Laws Of Fermentation,"* by William Patton. As of 1983, it could be obtained from Signal Press, 1730 Chicago Avenue, Evanston, Illinois 60201. More than a hundred years ago, this preacher was the only one in the town where he lived who believed in total abstinence. He saw that it was necessary to make an extensive study to see what scripture taught. This book is the result of that labor and is the very best thing I have ever read on the subject,

Now we come to the longest point in this entire study, but one which is most important, chiefly because so many insist that Jesus made and drank alcoholic wine.

19

8.   Jesus did not drink or make alcoholic wine.

Here are **ten proofs** from scripture:

The **first** reason is because of His holy nature. In Hebrews 7:26, we read that the Lord Jesus is *"holy, harmless, undefiled, separate from sinners."* No doubt, the Saviour, being God in the flesh, had an air of holiness about Himself that could be seen by even the most casual observer. For instance, the profane soldiers, who were sent to arrest Him, gave as their reason for returning without Him, that *"Never man spake like this man,"* (John 7:46) The words of Jesus were different: He, no doubt, had a very holy appearance, character, and speech.

Why is this so important? Consider this illustration. The word *cider* may mean alcoholic beverage, or plain apple juice. Suppose we lived during the 1920s, prohibition days, and were approached by two people offering us a drink of cider.

One of the persons, we knew to be one of the holiest men in town, faithful to the house of God, separated from the world, diligent in prayers, always witnessing to others; the other was a known liquor dealer. If each one offered us a drink of "his very own cider," we would assume that the holy person's was no more than apple juice, but there would be no doubt about our opinion regarding the liquor dealer's cider! Obviously, the character of a person influences what that one does.

Since the Lord Jesus Christ was *"holy, harmless, undefiled, separate from sinners,"* we may safely assume that He would not make that which is called in scripture a mocker and deceiver of man, causing untold misery.

A **second** reason: He would not contradict scripture. In Matthew 5:17-18, Christ made this clear, saying, *"Think not that I as come to destroy the law, or the prophets: I am not come to destroy, but to fulfill. For verily I say unto you, Till heaven and earth pass, one jot or one tittle shall in no wise pass from the law, till all be fulfilled."* Therefore, Christ could not have contradicted Habbakkuk 2:15, *"Woe unto him that givest his neighbor drink, that puttest thy bottle to him, and makest him drunken also, that thou mayest look on their nakedness!"*

Certainly, Jesus knew that this verse was in the Bible; He was well-acquainted with scripture, since it is His Word and was written about Him. He did not come to violate scripture, but to fulfill it. He could not have done so, if He had made alcoholic wine and given it to his neighbor!

Some people object to the use of this verse in this manner, by saying that it would apply only to one who would give his neighbor drink, for the purpose of looking on his nakedness. But we must remember: when one gives his neighbor drink which will make him drunk, he is putting himself in the very class of those who do so in order to look on their nakedness. And since the scripture commands us to *"abstain from all appearance of evil"* (1Thessalonians 5:22), we can be sure that the Lord Jesus would not have done something that would have been associated with such an evil practice as that described in Habakkuk 2:15. For the same reason, no Christian should be engaged in the selling of alcoholic beverage.

The **third** reason is that Leviticus 10:9-11 commands the priest of God, *"Do not drink wine nor strong drink...that ye may put difference between holy and unholy, and between unclean and clean ; and that ye may teach the children of*

Israel all the statutes which the Lord hath spoken ... " Now, since Hebrews 2:17 calls Christ *"a merciful and faithful high priest,"* we would expect Him to obey all scriptures pertaining to that office. If He had made or drunk alcoholic wine, He would have disobeyed these verses and would have been disqualified from teaching the children of Israel the statutes of the Lord.

The **fourth** reason is found in a passage which we have already considered: Proverbs 31:4-5 prohibits kings and princes from drinking alcoholic wine or any other strong drink. If they had done so, their judgment would have been perverted. It was necessary for Christ to obey these verses also, since He was Prince of Peace (Isaiah 9:6) and King of Kings (Revelation 19:16). In Matthew 27:11, He admitted to being the King of the Jews. He rode into Jerusalem on a donkey's colt, to fulfill Zechariah 9:9, which prophesied that Israel's king would enter the city in just that way. Undoubtedly, He was king, and as such, would have had to obey Proverbs 31:4-5

Reason **five**: Christ did not come to mock or deceive people, yet Proverbs 20:1 says that wine does both. Rather than coming to mock or deceive, He came to save!

Reason <u>six</u>: He did not come to send people to hell. We have already seen that Isaiah 5:11-14 teaches that hell had to be enlarged because of the drinking of alcoholic beverage. Christ did not come to send people to hell; listen to John 3;17: *"For God sent not his Son into the world to condemn the world; but that the world through him might be saved."*

Reason **seven**: Christ did not come to cast a stumblingblock before anyone; yet, Romans 14:21 teaches that a person who gives another alcoholic wine does just that. *"It is good neither to eat flesh, nor to drink wine, nor any thing whereby thy brother stumbleth, or is offended, or is made weak."* Everyone who has studied the problem of alcoholism has learned that some people can not handle any amount of alcohol, while others may drink one or two "social" drinks and stop. Experts do not know why this is true; various theories have been propounded, but nothing has been proved to be true regarding every person. Some say it is chemical; others insist that it must be psychological. The fact is, we do not know for certain. In any given group of people, there would be several potential alcoholics. What a shame it would be for a person, who is a potential slave to it, to get his first taste at the Lord's table in church, then proceed down the road of misery to an alcoholic's grave!

I certainly would not want my children to get their first taste of alcohol at the family meal; nor would I want them to get it at church. One or more of them could well be a potential alcoholic. As an evidence that this is possible, we should consider that some denominations which serve alcoholic wine in their religious services also operate homes for alcoholic priests!

But we can be absolutely sure that Christ did not come to cause others to stumble!

The **eighth** reason: John 2, the miracle of turning water into wine, does not require that it be alcoholic. Many insist that it was, on the basis of verse 10, which says, *"Every man at the beginning doth set forth good wine; and when men have well drunk, then that which is worse, but thou hast kept the good wine until now."* They would say that, in those days, it was common to serve the best alcoholic wine at first, saving the worst until later, when men's taste had been dulled by much drinking.

But the point is just the opposite here! These people could definitely recognize that the wine which Jesus made was much better than what they had been served at first. This could not have been possible, if they were already well on their way to becoming intoxicated! The fact is, neither the wine which they had at first, nor that which Christ made, was alcoholic.

Reason **nine** is found in the same passage: the Lord Jesus Christ would not have gotten glory from making drunk people drunker. Verse 11 is most important when it states that, by this miracle, Jesus *"manifested forth his glory."* Verse 10 indicates that the people had drunk quite a bit of whatever kind of wine they were drinking. If it had been alcoholic, they would have been intoxicated, or nearly so. Had Christ made alcoholic wine, He would have made drunk people drunker, or almost-drunk people completely drunk! Such a deed would certainly not have manifested any glory to Him!

This chapter also gives us the tenth reason: making drunk people drunker would not have caused his disciples to believe more strongly on him, yet verse 11 says that, as a result of what He did in turning the water into wine, *"his disciples believed on him."* John 1:41 shows that they had already believed on Him as Messiah; this was a deepening of their faith and a proof that they had not been wrong. Would making drunk people drunker inspire such faith? The opposite would be more likely! They were not looking for a Messiah who would pass out free booze! Thus, because of the description of this miracle and its result, we can not conclude otherwise than that this wine was non-alcoholic.

In closing, we must consider two things. One passage, we have already seen. Romans 14:21 clearly teaches that Christians should totally abstain, the reason being that it is good *"neither to eat flesh, nor to drink wine, nor any thing whereby thy brother stumbleth, or is offended, or is made weak."* We have already seen that people may be potential alcoholics. By the social drinking of alcohol, one might encourage a person to start drinking, who would not be able to stop. Missionaries and tourists to foreign countries, where alcohol is a common table beverage, should remember this. We should also wake up and realize that, in such countries, alcoholism is also rampant. Let us totally abstain, so that we might not encourage someone to drink and go down the road to alcoholism.

The last consideration is 1 Corinthians 6:9-10. Here, the Bible teaches that drunkenness will send a person to hell. *"Know ye not that the unrighteous shall not inherit the kingdom of God? Be not deceived: neither fornicators, nor idolaters, nor adulterers, nor effeminate, nor abusers of themselves with mankind, nor thieves, nor covetous, nor drunkards, nor revilers, nor extortioners, shall inherit the kingdom of God."*

This does not mean that a drunkard can never be saved, because the next verse says that some of the Corinthians committed these very acts before they were converted. A person can be gloriously set free from drunkenness, by receiving Jesus Christ as Lord and Saviour and by following His teachings. Many people have experienced such a release! But the tragedy is, that, if a person continues in drunkenness, refusing to let Jesus be the Lord, preferring rather to let king alcohol rule, that one can look for nothing but a drunkard's grave and eternity in the lake of fire. *"Be not deceived,"* the Bible says *"the unrighteous shall not inherit the kingdom of God."*

If you are having trouble with this sin, let me encourage you to realize that you can ask Jesus Christ to be the Lord of your life and Saviour from all your sins, and to set you free. You can know what it means to be free in Christ!

The Bible says, *"If the Son shall make you free, ye shall be free indeed,"* (John 8:36)

Realize that you are a sinner in God's sight, *"For all have sinned and come short of the glory of God,"* (Romans 3:23)

Repent of your rebellion against God, surrendering to His authority. *"Except ye repent, ye shall all likewise perish."* (Luke 13:3)

Receive Christ as your Lord and Saviour. *"As many as received him, to them gave he power to become the sons of God."* (John 1:12)

www.ingramcontent.com/pod-product-compliance
Lightning Source LLC
Chambersburg PA
CBHW071807020426
42331CB00008B/2419